5.50

# The
# Royal Navy
# in Old
# Photographs

# The
# Royal Navy
# in Old
# Photographs

**Wilfrid Pym Trotter** M.C.

Foreword by Richard Baker

J. M. DENT & SONS LTD   LONDON

First published 1975
© Wilfrid Pym Trotter 1975

Made in Great Britain

Filmset and printed by BAS Printers Limited
Wallop, Hampshire
for
J. M. DENT & SONS LTD
Aldine House · Albemarle Street · London

This book is set in Ehrhardt 453 10 on 11 pt
and 11 on 13 pt

ISBN 0 460 04132 0

# Foreword

by Richard Baker, Lieutenant-Commander, Royal Naval Reserve

Special enthusiasms are infectious, though they are not easily conveyed to those with an inbuilt resistance to them. Thus I have to admit I am not easily turned on by vintage cars, steam locomotives, Staffordshire pottery, stamps, coins, collections of cap badges or toy soldiers; but show me a ship, and I'm away—which is why I agreed so readily to contribute a Foreword to this book. It will delight confirmed ship addicts and surely create new ones.

Here is the most remarkable collection of ship photographs I have come across, presented with the kind of detailed information which delights an enthusiast. For no reason I could possibly explain, I like to know that the HMS *Donegal* of the 1850s had a funnel between the foremast and mainmast, while HMS *Sanspareil* had one between the mainmast and mizzen; that in 1867, HMS *Hector* was re-armed with two eight-inch and sixteen seven-inch muzzle-loading rifled guns; and that HMS *Inflexible*, launched in 1881, was the first ironclad to be lit by electricity and had armour twenty-four inches thick. I marvel at the ingenuity which created these seaborne fortresses, and wonder how they could possibly have stayed afloat: some of them, of course, didn't—like the top-heavy HMS *Captain*, which capsized and sank in September 1870 with the loss of 475 lives.

Though the great majority of sailors in those days happily did not drown, they lived out their lives in what we should consider great discomfort—and a great merit of this book is that it shows us the humans as well as the hardware of the old Royal Navy. How could they have stuck it? They had to, of course—discipline was harsh. But there was a measure of enjoyment too, even in the grim business of coaling ship, as you can see from some of the blackened faces portrayed in these pages. Intense competition grew up between the ships of a squadron, and between the Divisions of a ship, as the hungry monsters were fed in a matter of hours with the hundreds of tons of coal they needed to drive them through the ocean. For their speed, they depended on the sweat of the Stoker, stripped to the waist in almost unimaginable heat, noise and dirt down below. Yet the Stokers of HMS *Camperdown*, facing the camera in 1896, don't look in the least downcast. (In that same year, by the way, the crew of a Torpedo Boat Destroyer were pictured in their Duffel Coats. This was intriguing to one who glibly thought they came in with the convoys of World War Two.)

There wasn't much room for relaxation on the Lower Deck of that old Navy. There was the daily 'tot' of course, in the days before computer technology came along to confuse the sailor's brains—and I imagine Cutlass Drill must have made a welcome change from confinement in those great gun-turrets. Down below—just room to sling your hammock and take a quick look at *Answers* (see plate 110) before getting your head down for a few hours in an underventilated and absurdly overcrowded messdeck. The strange thing is that most of the sailors who still remember the pre-1914 Navy speak of it with pride and nostalgia.

There is, of course, a nostalgic appeal about this book: though we know conditions were hard, life in those days seemed—perhaps—to have more shape and purpose, and was somehow (or so we like to imagine) easier to understand. But photographs like these are fascinating chiefly because they act as triggers of the imagination; a whole way of life, long vanished, is suddenly suggested to the mind's eye; for a while we feel as those men must have felt, living and working in those strange floating Tanks of long ago.

Come to think of it, I do perfectly understand how pictures of old cars and trains, old coins and concert programmes can work the same kind of magic for some people; but for me (and surely many thousands of others) the sight of an old ship is far more potent. People like us will pore over Mr Trotter's unique collection for many a happy hour, in the company of one whose expertise and enthusiasm are indeed very special.

# Introduction

The popularity of the armed forces of the Crown waxes and wanes in relation to the danger of war with any formidable foreign power. When such a war breaks out nothing is too good for the sailors, the soldiers or the airmen; when peace is declared the love and admiration which the nation has borne for its defenders start rapidly to decline until in the course of a decade or two they are practically non-existent. The history of the present century has proved the truth of this, but whether or not it was equally true in the period covered by this book can only be discovered by considering the history of the country during that period.

The opening years of the nineteenth century were occupied with the Napoleonic Wars when the threat from across the Channel of a French invasion of our shores was ever present. The defeat of Napoleon's warships at Trafalgar in 1805 and of his armies at Waterloo ten years later brought peace at last, and as far as the Navy was concerned a rapid run down took place in the great armada which had comprised the British fleet and had saved the British nation. At this point we are confronted with a strange truth. The warships of 1815 were very like the warships of 1588, when the Spanish Armada had been destroyed. They were built of wood, their motive power was the wind of heaven, their method of communicating with one another was by hanging out different coloured flags amid the sails and the rigging, and their missiles were solid iron cannon balls propelled by gunpowder. Improvements of course there had been during the centuries, but these had all been of minor character.

The Napoleonic Wars left the British Navy undisputed mistress of the seas, and thus the duty of policing the oceans in both hemispheres devolved upon it. The Navy's first task was to rout out and destroy the three great Mohammedan strongholds of piracy and slavery in the Mediterranean, Tunis, Tripoli and Algiers. The two first towns yielded at once to the demands of Lord Exmouth, who commanded the British Mediterranean fleet, but Algiers put up a sturdy resistance, and it was only after a heavy bombardment that lasted all through one day and into the night that the Dey surrendered and gave up some twelve hundred Christian slaves whom he had held prisoner in his stronghold.

In October 1827, eleven years after this episode, the British, French and Russian fleets destroyed the Turkish and Egyptian fleets at the Battle of Navarino and thus secured the independence of Greece. Then in 1854 came the Crimean War, which lasted for two years and ended with the defeat of Russia by Great Britain and France. This war, the last naval struggle involving the Royal Navy in Europe in the nineteenth century, was a sanguinary one and called forth our utmost efforts both on land and on sea. By far the most important aspect of the naval campaign was the fact that towards the end of the War the capture of the Russian fortress of Kinburn was the scene of the first employment of armoured vessels in modern warfare, as well as the earliest operation in which steam vessels only were used. In addition to these two innovations the first effective use of mines, or torpedoes, or 'infernal machines', by which names they were popularly known, was made by the Russians in the Baltic operations of the Crimean War. So little seems to have been known by the naval officer of that day about explosives that we learn that when one of these unexploded 'infernal machines' was found by Rear Admiral Michael Seymour and his Flag Captain they hauled it into their gig and began to play with it. Not content with this, they took it aboard the Commander-in-Chief's flagship and again played with it until it exploded without, fortunately, any loss of life, but wounding half a dozen men including Admiral Seymour, who lost the sight of one eye.

The Treaty of Paris in 1856 ended the Crimean War and gave the British Admiralty the breathing space necessary to carry out the many innovations that had just been forced upon it by the realization that the wooden walls of England, which had won us so many naval battles in the past but whose motive power was provided only by the wind, were utterly outmoded by reason of the countless scientific discoveries and inventions of the age, and that in consequence the British Navy must be completely remodelled. For this reason, then, the year 1856 seems to be a reasonable date from which to start a book designed to show by a series of photographs what was happening to the Navy during the period in which occurred:

1. The transition from sail to steam propulsion.
2. The substitution of iron and steel for wood and consequently the introduction of armour.
3. The change from solid iron cannon balls to explosive shells.
4. The alteration in the position of a warship's main armament from inside the hull with the muzzles of the guns protruding through portholes, to the interior of one or more armoured turrets situated on the upper deck which, being on turntables, allowed the guns a greatly increased arc of fire.

The introduction of any of these revolutionary innovations would have presented difficulties of its own at any time. Because all of them were occurring at more or less the same time the difficulties were multiplied tenfold, since every one of them was dependent on one or more of the others. For example, the decks of the old sailing warships that still formed the fighting fleets of most of the world's navies in the middle of the nineteenth century were so cluttered both underfoot and aloft with ropes and spars that it was quite impossible to train a gun of any size other than on the lower decks through portholes.

Before a start could be made on the fourth innovation therefore it was necessary to clear away all the paraphernalia incidental to sailing and proceed with the first innovation by installing engines.

Despite all the difficulties that presented themselves the Admiralty got down with vigour to the job in hand, and during the next thirty years produced a large number of battleships and cruisers, many of which were definitely on the right road, but a few of which were difficult to justify as successful warships from any angle. Although by their wise policy of not repeating the prototypes of the experiments which they had produced the Admiralty spared the Navy from the disaster of possessing a fleet of warships all suffering from the same faults, nevertheless at the end of the eighteen-eighties Britain awoke to the realization that her Navy was a heterogeneous collection, practically every ship of which differed in speed and armament from every other ship, and could therefore be of little use to its commander-in-chief, being almost unmanageable as a fleet not only to fight an action but even to steam together at sea.

The realization that, despite progress in the modernization of the Navy, the fleet was unready to take on the task of defending the Empire in the event of a major war came as a shock to the British people, and in 1889 the premier, Lord Salisbury, was able to introduce and pass a Naval Defence Act which provided for the building of ten battle-ships, nine first-class cruisers, twenty-nine second-class cruisers, four third-class cruisers, and eighteen torpedo gunboats at a total cost of £21,500,000.

The years spent in trials and experiments had shown the naval architects the types of warships necessary for the next decade or two, and the Naval Defence Act gave them the opportunity to concentrate on producing standard designs of different classes, with gradual improvements in each class.

By the early years of the present century several events had occurred which considerably influenced the whole question of defence. The first of these was the improvement in the relationship between England and France, largely brought about by King Edward VII. The second was an Anglo-Russian Convention in 1907 which did much to remove the threat of Russia as a possible opponent of Great Britain, a position which she had held alternatively with France for a number of years; and the third was the growing animosity of Germany, whose desire for an empire was becoming fanned to fever heat by the personal jealousy of her Emperor Wilhelm. The Kaiser, always interested in naval and military matters, had, during the course of several visits to his grandmother Queen Victoria, seen the British Fleet (of which he had been appointed an admiral) and now he had become determined that Germany should possess a large Navy built on British lines.

Fortunately for this country the popularity of the armed forces was on the up and up, and Parliament had little difficulty in finding the money needed.

In 1906 an important event occurred: Admiral of the Fleet Lord Fisher, the then First Sea Lord, introduced the 'all big gun' ship. Built in the greatest secrecy and in a record short time, HMS *Dreadnought*, by reason of her startling innovations, including the increase of her main armament from the usual four to ten 12-inch guns and the fact that she was the first turbine-driven battleship, *immediately* made all other battleships throughout the world out of date and of minor use. This might have created a serious situation for this country because Britain, which had kept well ahead of the German efforts, was by the launch of this revolutionary ship at once deprived of every advantage, and the armaments race had to be started again from scratch. By this time, however, the nation, alarmed by the growing certainty that war was not far away, was more ardently enthusiastic than ever, and for the next eight years a staggering number of warships of all types were produced, enabling Great Britain to enter the First World War greatly superior to Germany in naval power.

This large increase in the size of the Navy emphasized the fact that most of the names allotted to new warships were repetitions of old ones, many of them borne by ships that had won fame for themselves in various actions in the past. This led to the adoption, albeit unofficially at that period, of battle honours, and both factors furthered the continuity of the traditions of the Royal Navy that are so bound up in the histories of its ships. Wood and sail give way to steel and steam but a ship is immortal; when she becomes obsolete and is broken up her spirit remains and some day will enter into a newly launched hull that bears her name and invest the new addition to the fleet with the lustre won in an earlier life.

W.P.T.

# Acknowledgments

Plates 27, 51 and 147 are reproduced by permission of the Imperial War Museum.

Plates 7, 89, 99, 101, 110–13, 115–20, 123, 124, 126–8 are reproduced by permission of the National Maritime Museum, London.

# Ironclad battleships built for the Royal Navy between 1860 and 1914

IRON BROADSIDE SHIPS

| | | |
|---|---|---|
| *Warrior* | launched 1860 | (still exists as an oil hulk) |
| *Black Prince* | 1861 | |
| *Defence* | 1861 | |
| *Resistance* | 1861 | |
| *Hector* | 1862 | |
| *Valiant* | 1862 | |
| *Achilles* | 1863 | |
| *Minotaur* | 1863 | } Five-masted |
| *Agincourt* | 1865 | |
| *Northumberland* | 1866 | |

WOODEN BROADSIDE SHIPS

The sides of these ships were covered with iron but they were actually built of wood to use up surplus supplies of timber.

| | |
|---|---|
| *Caledonia* | 1862 |
| *Ocean* | 1863 |
| *Prince Consort* | 1863 |
| *Royal Oak* | 1863 |
| *Royal Alfred* | 1864 |
| *Lord Clyde* | 1864 |
| *Zealous* | 1864 |
| *Lord Warden* | 1865 |
| *Repulse* | 1868 |

SMALL ARMOURED WARSHIPS

| | |
|---|---|
| *Research* | 1863 |
| *Enterprise* | 1864 |
| *Favorite* | 1864 |
| *Pallas* | 1865 |

CENTRAL BATTERY SHIPS

| | |
|---|---|
| *Bellerophon* | 1865 |

| | | |
|---|---|---|
| *Penelope* | launched | 1867 |
| *Hercules* | | 1868 |
| *Audacious* | | 1869 |
| *Invincible* | | 1869 |
| *Vanguard* | | 1869 |
| *Iron Duke* | | 1870 |
| *Sultan* | | 1870 |
| *Swiftsure* | | 1870 |
| *Triumph* | | 1870 |
| *Alexandra* | | 1875 |
| *Superb* | | 1875 |
| *Belleisle* | | 1876 |
| *Temeraire* | | 1876 |
| *Orion* | | 1879 |

TURRET SHIPS

| | |
|---|---|
| *Royal Sovereign* | 1857 |
| *Scorpion* | 1863 |
| *Wivern* | 1863 |
| *Prince Albert* | 1864 |
| *Cerberus* | 1868 |
| *Monarch* | 1868 |
| *Captain* | 1869 |
| *Abyssinia* | 1870 |
| *Hotspur* | 1870 |
| *Magdala* | 1870 |
| *Cyclops* | 1871 |
| *Devastation* | 1871 |
| *Glatton* | 1871 |
| *Gorgon* | 1871 |
| *Hecate* | 1871 |
| *Hydra* | 1871 |
| *Rupert* | 1872 |
| *Thunderer* | 1872 |
| *Neptune* | 1874 |
| *Dreadnought* | 1875 |
| *Inflexible* | 1876 |
| *Agamemnon* | 1879 |
| *Ajax* | 1880 |

BATTLESHIPS

| | |
|---|---|
| *Conqueror* | 1881 |
| *Hero* | 1885 |
| *Colossus* | 1882 |
| *Edinburgh* | 1882 |

| | | |
|---|---|---|
| *Collingwood* | launched 1882 | ⎫ |
| *Rodney* | 1884 | |
| *Benbow* | 1885 | |
| *Camperdown* | 1885 | ⎬ Admiral class |
| *Howe* | 1885 | |
| *Anson* | 1886 | ⎭ |
| | | |
| *Sanspareil* | 1887 | |
| *Victoria* | 1887 | |
| | | |
| *Trafalgar* | 1887 | |
| *Nile* | 1888 | |
| | | |
| *Barfleur* | 1892 | |
| *Centurion* | 1892 | |
| | | |
| *Empress of India* | 1891 | ⎫ |
| *Hood* | 1891 | |
| *Royal Sovereign* | 1891 | |
| *Ramillies* | 1892 | |
| *Repulse* | 1892 | ⎬ Royal Sovereign class |
| *Resolution* | 1892 | |
| *Revenge* | 1892 | |
| *Royal Oak* | 1892 | ⎭ |
| | | |
| *Renown* | 1895 | |
| | | |
| *Caesar* | 1896 | ⎫ |
| *Hannibal* | 1896 | |
| *Illustrious* | 1896 | |
| *Jupiter* | 1895 | |
| *Magnificent* | 1894 | ⎬ Majestic class |
| *Majestic* | 1895 | |
| *Mars* | 1896 | |
| *Prince George* | 1895 | |
| *Victorious* | 1895 | ⎭ |
| | | |
| *Albion* | 1898 | ⎫ |
| *Canopus* | 1897 | |
| *Glory* | 1899 | |
| *Goliath* | 1898 | ⎬ Canopus class |
| *Ocean* | 1898 | |
| *Vengeance* | 1899 | ⎭ |
| | | |
| *Bulwark* | 1899 | ⎫ |
| *Formidable* | 1898 | |
| *Implacable* | 1899 | |
| *Irresistible* | 1898 | |
| *London* | 1899 | ⎬ Formidable class |
| *Prince of Wales* | 1902 | |
| *Queen* | 1902 | |
| *Venerable* | 1899 | ⎭ |

| | | |
|---|---|---|
| *Albemarle* | launched 1901 | ⎫ |
| *Cornwallis* | 1901 | ⎪ |
| *Duncan* | 1901 | ⎪ |
| *Exmouth* | 1901 | ⎬ Duncan class |
| *Montagu* | 1901 | ⎪ |
| *Russell* | 1901 | ⎭ |

| | |
|---|---|
| *Swiftsure* | 1903 |
| *Triumph* | 1903 |

| | | |
|---|---|---|
| *Africa* | 1905 | ⎫ |
| *Britannia* | 1904 | ⎪ |
| *Commonwealth* | 1903 | ⎪ |
| *Dominion* | 1903 | ⎪ |
| *Hibernia* | 1905 | ⎬ King Edward VII class |
| *Hindustan* | 1903 | ⎪ |
| *King Edward VII* | 1903 | ⎪ |
| *New Zealand* | 1904 | ⎪ |
| renamed *Zealandia* in 1911 | | ⎭ |

| | |
|---|---|
| *Agamemnon* | 1906 |
| *Lord Nelson* | 1906 |

| | |
|---|---|
| *Dreadnought* | 1906 |

| | | | |
|---|---|---|---|
| *Bellerophon* | 1907 | ⎫ | ⎫ |
| *Superb* | 1907 | ⎬ Bellerophon | ⎪ |
| *Temeraire* | 1907 | ⎭ class | ⎪ improved |
| *Collingwood* | 1908 | ⎫ | ⎬ *Dreadnoughts* |
| *St Vincent* | 1908 | ⎬ St Vincent | ⎪ |
| *Vanguard* | 1909 | ⎭ class | ⎭ |

| | | |
|---|---|---|
| *Colossus* | 1910 | ⎫ |
| *Hercules* | 1910 | ⎬ Colossus class |
| *Neptune* | 1909 | ⎭ |

| | | |
|---|---|---|
| *Conqueror* | 1911 | ⎫ |
| *Monarch* | 1911 | ⎪ |
| *Orion* | 1910 | ⎬ Orion class |
| *Thunderer* | 1911 | ⎭ |

| | | |
|---|---|---|
| *Ajax* | 1912 | ⎫ |
| *Audacious* | 1912 | ⎪ |
| *Centurion* | 1911 | ⎬ King George V class |
| *King George V* | 1911 | ⎭ |

| | | |
|---|---|---|
| *Benbow* | 1913 | ⎫ |
| *Emperor of India* | 1913 | ⎪ |
| *Iron Duke* | 1912 | ⎬ Iron Duke class |
| *Marlborough* | 1912 | ⎭ |

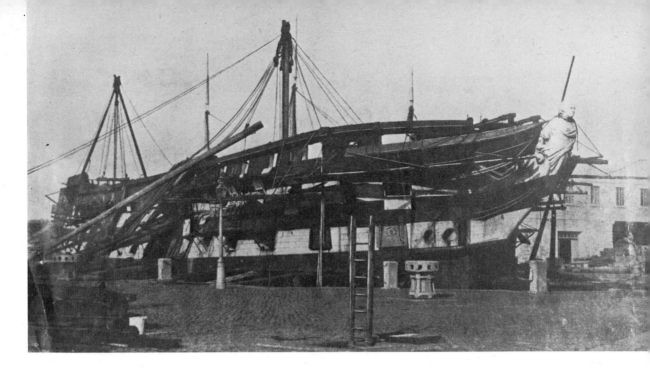

1. The *San Josef*, a Spanish first-rate of 112 guns, boarded and captured personally by Commodore Horatio Nelson during the Battle of Cape St Vincent in 1797, served in the Royal Navy until she was broken up at Devonport Dockyard in 1849. This view of her just prior to her demolition is reputed to be the earliest photograph of one of H.M. ships.

2. HMS *Hibernia* in dry dock, Malta. This fine old sailing battleship, a first-rate carrying 110 guns, was launched in 1804. After spending most of her active life as the Flagship of the Mediterranean Fleet she became the Flagship of the Base at Malta in 1855. She was sold and broken up in 1902.

3. Two obsolete first-rates of the 1850s, *Duke of Wellington* (right) and *Marlborough* (left) spending their last years as depot ships at Portsmouth Dockyard. It is on record that to build HMS *Duke of Wellington*—250 feet long with a 60-foot beam—an oak forest of seventy-six acres was cleared of trees. In this photograph, taken about 1898, a drum and fife band leads ratings ashore from the two hulks.

4. The principal establishments for training boys for the Navy in the second half of the nineteenth century were at Portsmouth, Devonport and Portland. HMS *St Vincent*, a first-rate built in 1815, became a training ship in 1862 at Portsmouth; she was sold and broken up in 1906.

5. HMS *Sanspareil* (left) and HMS *Donegal*. The introduction of steam in the 1850s was viewed with some disquiet and the Admiralty was forced to retain masts and sails against the possibility of machinery breakdowns. Mechanical devices for raising propellers out of the water and lowering funnels to deck level were introduced. The lowered funnel of *Sanspareil* is between the mainmast and mizzen mast, that of *Donegal* between foremast and mainmast.

6.  No fewer than 158 screw gunboats, built of wood, similar to HMS *Magnet* here depicted, were constructed for service in the Crimean War.

7.  One of the officers and a number of ratings of the screw gunboat *Coquette*, launched 1855.

8.  The Grand Harbour, Malta, about 1862, showing a part of the Mediterranean Fleet.

9.   Despite appearances, HMS *Jackal* was an iron paddle gun-vessel, built at Glasgow in 1844. She served in the Royal Navy hunting down pirates and slavers on the west coast of Africa, and was sold in November 1887.

10.   HMS *Warrior*, launched in December 1860, was the first armour-clad warship in the world to be built entirely of iron. 'I often wonder', the First Lord of the Admiralty remarked to her builder, 'how I mustered sufficient courage to order the construction of such a novel vessel.' 'I often wonder', replied her builder, 'how I mustered sufficient courage to undertake it.' Seen here in 1876, *Warrior* is still afloat doing duty as a naval oil storage ship in Pembroke Dock, Milford Haven.

11. HMS *Warrior* and her sister ship *Black Prince* were quickly followed by two other pairs of ironclads, *Defence* and *Resistance*, and *Hector* and *Valiant*. HMS *Hector*, whose deck is seen in this view taken from her foretop, spent the last years of her life as part of the *Vernon* torpedo school, when she was the first ship fitted with wireless telegraphy. She was sold in 1905.

12. Some of the officers of HMS *Hector* in 1884. At that time the curl in the top row of gold braid was worn only by a warship's executive officers. The Captain is the third from the right.

13. Originally armed with four 7-inch breech-loading guns and twenty 68-pounders, HMS *Hector* was re-armed in 1867 with two 8-inch and sixteen 7-inch muzzle-loading rifled guns. A gun's crew are here seen on deck.

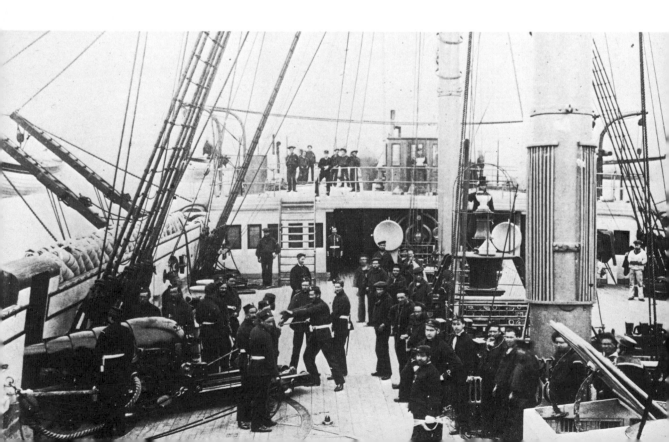

14. The foredeck of HMS *Minotaur*. Built at Blackwall and launched in 1863, she was one of the early armoured ironclads. On the left is a senior officer mounting the steps leading to the binnacle platform, while on the platform is a civilian, probably an Admiralty expert come aboard to swing the ship for compasses.

15. On the afterdeck of HMS *Minotaur* we see one of the 8-inch muzzle-loading rifled guns that formed part of her main armament.

16. By the time that the five-masted armoured battleships *Agincourt*, *Minotaur* and *Northumberland* were built in the mid 1860s the age-old type of figurehead was no longer being fitted on the largest ships. Henceforward their bows were adorned by an ornate scroll of varied design, as shown here on HMS *Agincourt*.

17. The earliest ironclads were broadside ships, their large guns being fired through portholes on either side. HMS *Bellerophon*, completed in 1866, ushered in a type of battleship with a short hull carrying a small number of the heaviest guns in a central battery located over a waterline belt of armour. *Bellerophon* is seen here under sail and steam as the Flagship of the North America and West Indies station, her last commission overseas after twenty-six years' service.

18. One of the 6-inch breech-loaders aft and the rifle racks aboard HMS *Bellerophon*, c. 1885.

19. The battery of 8-inch breech-loaders on the main deck of HMS *Bellerophon*, c. 1885.

20. The battleship *Triumph* and her sister ship the *Swiftsure* were specially designed for service in the Pacific where long distances called for high cruising performance under sail and adequate speed for fighting under steam. After service in the Channel and Mediterranean Fleets HMS *Triumph* served as Flagship in the Pacific from 1878 to 1888.

21. HMS *Royal Sovereign*, originally laid down in 1849 as a 131-gun three-decker wooden steam battleship, was launched in 1857 but in 1862 was cut down to her lower deck and finished, in 1864, as an armoured turret ship. She was thus the first British turret ship to be completed and the only one to have a timber hull, an experiment not repeated. She was armed with five 10-inch $12\frac{1}{2}$-ton muzzle-loading guns housed in four rotating turrets, two guns being in the foremost turret before the funnel. All guns were able to fire on either beam.

22. HMS *Rosario*, seen here in Sydney Harbour, was a wooden screw sloop built at Deptford and launched in 1860. Her first commission was in the West Indies hunting down slavers off Cuba, her next two on the Australia station, 1866–74.

23. HMS *Druid*, a wooden screw corvette of
1869, the last warship built at Deptford; here
photographed about 1875, she was sold in
1886.

24. HMS *Captain*, designed by Captain
Cowper Coles R.N. and built by Lairds at
Birkenhead, was an ironclad turret ship.
Her armament consisted of four 12-inch
muzzle-loading rifled guns in two circular
turrets widely separated on the centre line;
one of the turrets can be seen here.

25. One of several peculiarities of HMS
*Captain* was the fact that she was the only
two-decked battleship in the Royal Navy.
Her upper deck (shown here) consisted of a
forecastle and a poop connected by a flying
deck. Throughout the three years of her
construction serious differences of opinion
arose concerning her stability, since although
her masts and sails were as heavy as those in
other battleships she had a freeboard of less
than 9 feet. Misgivings were justified when
during a gale on the night of 6th September
1870 she capsized and went to the bottom,
carrying with her all but eighteen of those on
board. Among the 475 people who perished
were her Commanding Officer, Captain
Burgoyne V.C., and her designer.

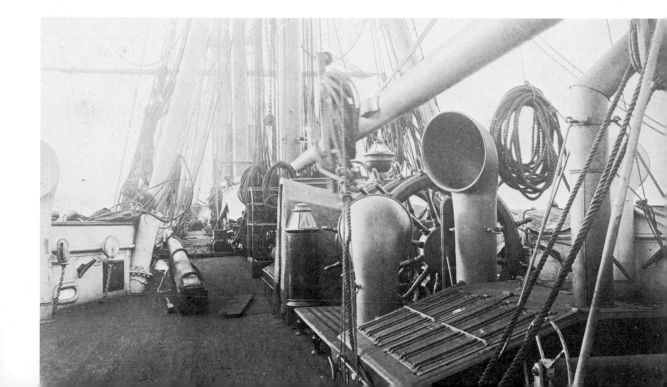

26.   The terrible disaster that overtook HMS *Captain* condemned for ever the turret ship with heavy rigging and a low freeboard. HMS *Devastation* and her two sister ships *Thunderer* (Pls. 34, 77) and *Dreadnought* (Pl. 43), built in the early 1870s, were turret ships but in them for the first time sails had entirely disappeared. One of *Devastation*'s twelve-inch guns in its turret can be seen in the centre of the photograph.

27.   On 5th July 1872 the breastwork monitor *Glatton*, considered one of the best protected vessels of her day, was fired at by HMS *Hotspur* to test her turret armour. Two rounds of 12-inch projectiles fired at a range of 200 yards scored hits but without impairing the efficiency of the turret. The effects of the test were examined by *Glatton*'s designer, Mr E. J. Read, seen here on the left in a hat and black coat.

28.   Battleships of the Channel Squadron lying off Lisbon, December 1885. Left, *Iron Duke* (nearer) and *Monarch*; right, *Agincourt* (nearer) and *Minotaur*.

29. Four battleships of the Mediterranean Fleet at Malta, 1874. Nearest is HMS *Research*, behind her lies *Invincible* with the Flagship *Lord Warden* behind her; farthest away is probably HMS *Swiftsure*.

30. A lieutenant and three junior officers of the iron broadside battleship *Achilles* grouped round the 9-inch gun at the stern which formed part of the new armament that she received in 1874.

31. Portsmouth Harbour. Naval ships dressed overall, possibly for Queen Victoria's Golden Jubilee in 1887.

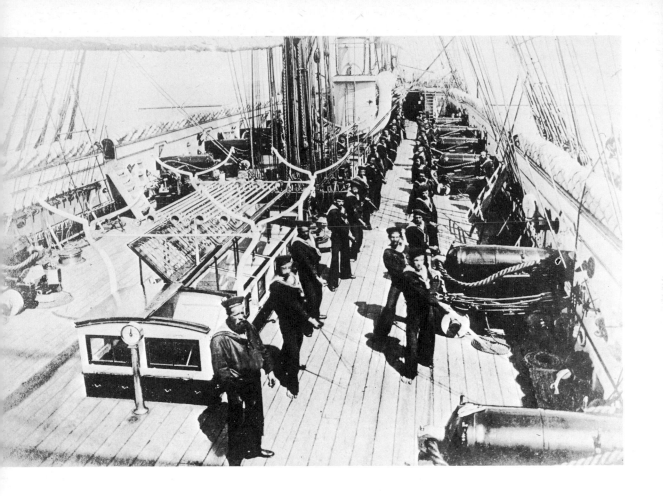

32. Cutlass drill on the deck of the wooden screw corvette *Sapphire* in 1878, in Australian waters. Note the loosely fitting jumpers worn in those days.

33. With her two masts and raking bell-topped funnels the handsome wooden paddle despatch vessel *Salamis* was well known in the Mediterranean Fleet for the twenty years of her life, which ended at Sheerness in 1883.

34. Five battleships of the Mediterranean Fleet at anchor in Malta Harbour about 1882. Left foreground, *Thunderer*, behind her, *Invincible*; centre, *Alexandra*, almost hiding *Rupert*; right, *Monarch*.

35. The cruiser *Calliope* leaving Sydney in 1890, after a commission in which she had earned fame by escaping from the harbour of Apia in Samoa in the teeth of a hurricane, forging her way to the comparative safety of the open sea. Three German and three American warships in harbour were destroyed or driven ashore. The nickname 'Hurricane Jumper' stuck to her throughout her later life.

36. HMS *Melita* was the only one of her class of six steam sloops to be built abroad. Launched in Malta in 1888, she served with the Mediterranean Fleet until coming to England to be paid off at Devonport in 1902. She then served fourteen years as a Boom Defence vessel.

37. HMS *Ringdove*, a typical late nineteenth-century gunboat.

38. HMS *Inflexible*, completed in June 1881 over seven years after she was laid down, was unique. Her 24-inch armour was thicker than that of any ironclad before or since; her four 16-inch 81-ton muzzle-loading guns were housed in two turrets amidships placed *en echelon*; her 60-foot torpedo boats were stowed on her after superstructure; there were two submerged torpedo tubes in her bows while additional torpedo launching gear was fitted at bow and stern, the former a 'scoop' down which the torpedo ran when released, the latter an arrangement of tall sheers by which torpedoes could be thrown out; finally, she was the first ironclad to be lit by electricity.

39. Belief in the possibility of steam-powered ships ramming each other in war gave rise to the 'armoured ram', and two experimental vessels were built, *Hotspur* and *Rupert*, completed in the early 1870s. Neither was a success, however. During reconstruction in 1887 HMS *Hotspur* was fitted with an early type of torpedo net: cumbersome nets were slung along the side with a single boom projecting from the stem, but this form of protection could not be used when under way and was removed after a few years (see also Pl. 175).

40–2. One of the strangest experiments in the latter half of the nineteenth century was undoubtedly HMS *Polyphemus*, a 'torpedo ram' intended to accompany a squadron of battleships in a protective capacity. Built at Chatham, she was launched in June 1881 and completed the following February; for the next three years she was subjected to a series of trials and experiments and numerous alterations were carried out in her. She proved a poor seaboat and no other ship of her type was built. In June and July 1885 *Polyphemus* formed part of a large squadron which carried out off the coast of Ireland the first Naval Manœuvres ever attempted on a big scale. During these operations she successfully charged a boom constructed to protect the fleet in Bantry Bay, passing right over it without sustaining any damage.

43.  HMS *Dreadnought*, decks cleared for action, at Malta *c.* 1888, with one of the Indian troopships in the background.

44.  HMS *Ajax* (shown here) and *Agamemnon* were two of the most unsatisfactory battleships ever built for the Royal Navy. Reduced editions of *Inflexible* (Pl. 38), they exaggerated that ship's defects without possessing her virtues. They were poor seaboats, suffering from excessive beam and a tendency to lurch and plunge heavily in a seaway, and were dangerous to manœuvre in company at over 10 knots.

45.  The decorated stern of the cruiser *Katoomba*. She was one of a special squadron of five cruisers and two torpedo gunboats built to operate exclusively in Australasian waters, arriving there in 1891. The colonial governments of Australia contributed to the cost and upkeep of the squadron, which was one result of the Colonial Conference of 1887.

46. HMS *Victoria* was built as *Renown* but renamed prior to her launch in April 1887 to mark the impending Golden Jubilee of Queen Victoria. In 1890 she was commissioned as Flagship of the Mediterranean Fleet and in the photograph is wearing the Admiral's flag. On 22nd June 1893 during fleet exercises off Tripoli she was rammed and sunk by HMS *Camperdown*. Admiral Tryon, 22 officers and 336 ratings lost their lives.

47. The second-class cruiser *Arethusa*, launched in 1882, served on the Mediterranean station 1893–6; during that time experiments were made with a new explosive called Lyddite. This illustration of *Arethusa* carrying out a practice shoot is said to record the first occasion when Lyddite was used.

48. The destroyers *Sparrowhawk*, temporarily wearing a Rear Admiral's flag, and *Virago* at Esquimalt, British Columbia, in the 1890s. In 1903 they were transferred to the China Station and a year later *Sparrowhawk* struck an uncharted rock near the mouth of the Yangtse-Kiang and sank; no lives were lost and the guns and gear were saved.

49. First-class Torpedo Boat No. 56, one of a group of twenty launched in 1886, at Malta about 1899. The muzzles of two of her four deck torpedo tubes can be seen behind the member of the crew standing with his feet apart.

50. Torpedo boats were considered by senior naval officers of the day to be a formidable threat to the battleship and the cruiser. About 1889 therefore a class of well-armed, fast 'torpedo-boat catchers' was conceived; they were not a success as such. One of the early vessels of this type, HMS *Sandfly*, is seen here.

51. One of the earliest torpedo boat destroyers, HMS *Ardent* was launched in 1894. In 1904 vessels of the Russian Baltic fleet, which was sailing to the Far East to take part in the Russo–Japanese War, opened fire on British trawlers. *Ardent* and a number of other destroyers were at once sent to shadow the fleet.

52. HMS *Jason*, a typical torpedo gunboat launched in 1892, was a smart little vessel that spent her whole life in United Kingdom waters. In 1909 she became one of the earliest minesweepers of the Royal Navy.

53.  *Takaroa*, one of the early second-class torpedo boats maintained by the Australians towards the end of the century.

54.  Second-class Torpedo Boat No. 96, one of many designed to be carried on the decks of battleships. No. 96 is here aboard HMS *Camperdown*, the flagship of a Rear Admiral whose flag is painted on her hull.

55.  In 1885 the Royal Navy took over from Chile two torpedo boats recently built in England. Torpedo Boat No. 39 is seen here at Esquimalt, where she served with Torpedo Boat No. 40 for a number of years in the defence of the Pacific coast of Canada.

56. HMS *Trafalgar* and her sister ship *Nile*, laid down in 1886 and completed in 1890–1, were the last of the single-citadel turret battleships and the heaviest British battleships to that date (displacement 11,940 tons). *Trafalgar* originally had short funnels but in 1891 these were raised by 17 feet.

57.  HMS *Trafalgar* was the flagship of the Rear Admiral Second in Command of the Mediterranean Fleet from 1890 to 1896. Rear Admiral Markham and his staff are here photographed with the officers of *Trafalgar*, including the chaplain, on her quarter-deck. Behind the group is the turret housing two of the four 13·5-inch guns which formed the ship's main armament.

58.  The sloop *Torch* and gunboats *Ringdove* and *Goldfinch* astern of her in dry dock at Cockatoo Island, Sydney, in April 1897.

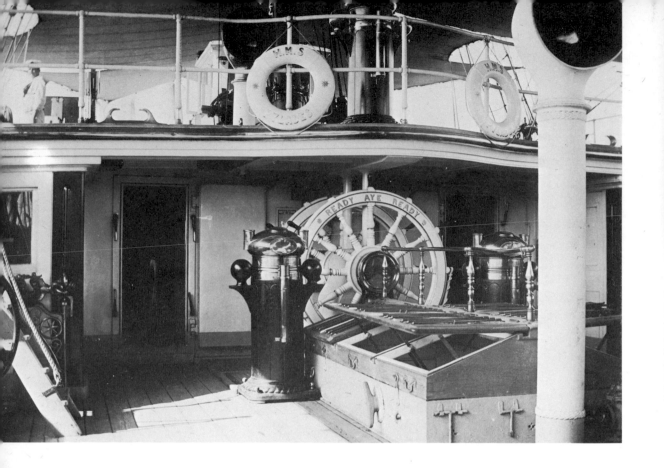

59–61. HMS *Pylades*, a composite screw
steam corvette built at Sheerness in 1884,
here photographed in 1897. (Above) One of
the steering wheels with a binnacle on either
side. (Above right) The starboard battery;
even at this date the upper decks of some warships still had high bulwarks similar to those
of a century earlier. (Below right) The sail-
maker repairing the ship's paying-off pendant.

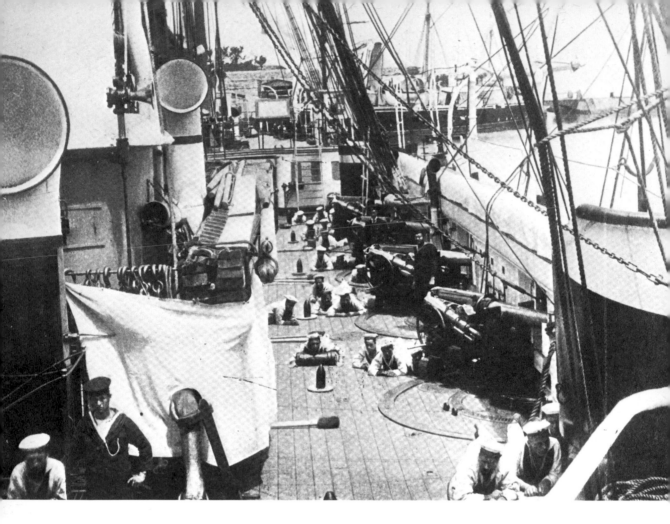

62. Carrying out the exercise 'prepare to ram' aboard the screw corvette *Tourmaline* about 1880.

63. Cutlass drill on the quarterdeck of HMS *Resolution*, 1896.

64. Stokers of HMS *Camperdown* in 1896.

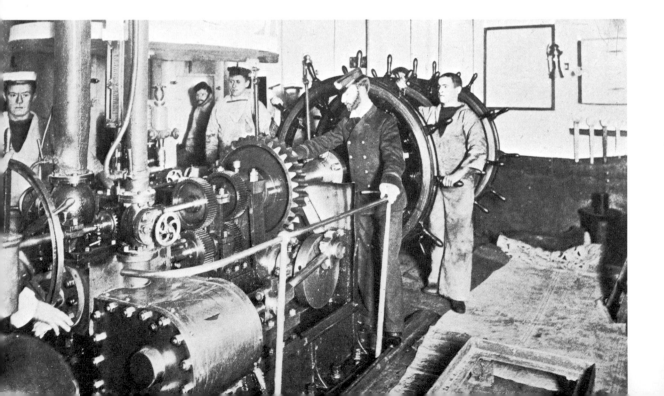

65.    In the engine room of HMS *Resolution*, about 1896.

66.    Steam steering gear aboard HMS *Resolution*, 1896.

67.    Petty Officers of the cruiser *Blake* in the 1890s. When confirmed in his rank after a year the petty officer exchanged his seaman's dress ('square rig') for a suit, collar and tie and peaked cap (known as 'fore and aft rig'). The badge of rank, on the left arm, is two crossed anchors surmounted by a crown.

68. Stowing an anchor on the deck of the cruiser *Theseus*, 1896. One of her two 9·2-inch guns is seen at the right; she was launched at Thames Ironworks in 1892.

69. A searchlight on the bridge of HMS *Magnificent*.

70. A steam launch attached to HMS *Vernon*, the torpedo school at Portsmouth. She was used for experimental work with spar torpedoes, weapons proved to have enormous possibilities during the American Civil War but eventually discarded in favour of Whitehead torpedoes fired through tubes.

71. Warheads for Whitehead torpedoes being taken along the dock to a ship.

72. Some of the crew of the torpedo-boat destroyer *Sturgeon* in 1896. The early destroyers were not comfortable and the duffel coat made its appearance to bring some warmth to a cold job.

73. HMS *Bullfinch*, a torpedo-boat destroyer launched in 1898. One of the C class, she had a displacement of 370 tons and speed of 30 knots. Here she is passing along Southsea front on her way into Portsmouth Harbour.

74. Naval cadets on board their training ship, HMS *Britannia*, in 1895. Here they received a general education as well as the specialized training necessary for their future career. They are grouped round a binnacle, the stand in which was fixed a compass bowl and from which they learned the mysteries of navigation.

75. The midshipmen aboard HMS *Howe* receiving seamanship instruction with the aid of one of the ship's boats rigged as a fully rigged three-masted vessel.

76. Instruction in the working of a torpedo for cadets aboard the cruiser *Theseus*.

77. HMS *Thunderer* and her sister ships (see Pls. 26 and 43) carried their main armament in turrets with clear end-on as well as broadside arcs of fire. Their design was in fact revolutionary and at first evoked hostile criticism, but this gave way to admiration when the ships proved safe and seaworthy and fulfilled the intentions of their design. Photographed in 1898.

78. Launched in 1886, *Narcissus* was a belted cruiser—that is, she had a belt of armour to protect the most vulnerable parts of her hull. The photograph of 1898 shows her quarterdeck, on which was mounted one of her two 9·2-inch guns.

79.  HMS *Kite* was one of twenty-five twin-screw iron gunboats built in the 1870s and known as 'flat-irons'. With a length of 85 feet and a beam of 26 feet these vessels proved very steady gun-platforms and several of them were attached to the Naval Gunnery Schools.

80.  The *Drudge* was built towards the end of the century as a gunboat, but was used for a number of years entirely to test guns of different calibre.

81.  The main armament of the seven battle-ships of the 'Royal Sovereign' class of the 1890s consisted of four 13·5-inch guns, two on the forecastle and two on the quarterdeck. The photograph shows the forecastle guns of HMS *Royal Sovereign* in 1895.

82. Morning prayers abaft the quarterdeck 12-inch guns of HMS *Magnificent*.

83. Loading drill with a 6-inch quick-firing gun on the deck of the battleship *Resolution* in 1896.

84. Drill with a light gun on board the battleship *Camperdown*: a landing party ready to go ashore. In charge is a bearded petty officer with three good conduct stripes surmounted by the badge of his rank.

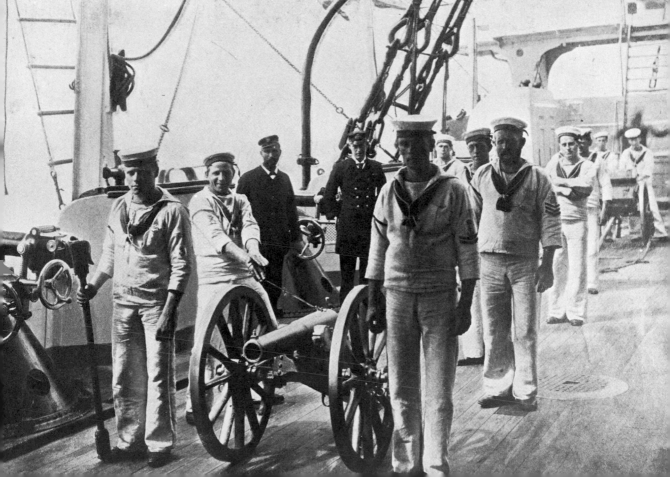

85. Instructors at Whale Island, the Portsmouth gunnery school, practising with a Maxim machine gun, 1895.

86. Naval training ashore, 1896: a landing party forms a rallying point to act as a resistance square.

87. HMS *Doris* was one of a class of nine second-class cruisers of 5,600-tons displacement built between 1894 and 1896. Here she has a number of canvas ventilating cowls rigged in place of the more usual metal ones.

88. The handsome little second-class cruiser HMS *Marathon*, 2,950 tons displacement. In 1900 on the outbreak of the 'Boxer' Rising she was hurriedly sent from the East Indies to the China Station. This photograph, of about that period, shows her under way with a lookout half way up her foremast while at either end of the bridge ratings are heaving the lead.

89.   Recruiting in the west of England.

90.   Gymnastics aboard the battleship *Howe* in the 1890s.

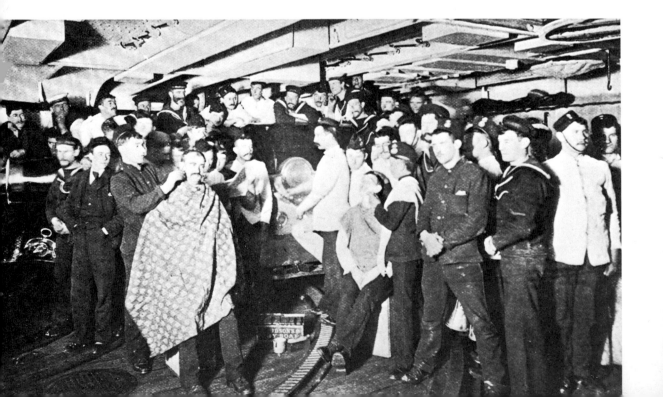

91. Lack of space did not prevent the blue-jacket of eighty or so years ago from enjoying his leisure. A friendly boxing match was always a favourite hobby even though there was seldom a ring and usually only a handful of his pals to applaud.

92. The barber aboard a battleship in the 1890s.

93. In 1895 the ship's mascot of HMS *Magnificent* was a tame bear, which lived aboard.

94, 95.  Pay day is always welcome! It was usual, though apparently not in the ship above left, photographed about 1890, for Jack to remove his cap for the paymaster to place his money on top of it. In the lower photograph a petty officer with two good conduct stripes but not yet confirmed in his rank receives his pay aboard HMS *Royal Sovereign* about the time that she was paid off in 1895 after serving a three-year commission as Flagship of the Channel Squadron.

96.  A dockyard repair party (and 'crew') on board the third-class cruiser *Philomel*, about 1900.

97.   Her Majesty Queen Victoria
in the royal yacht, the second
*Victoria and Albert*, a paddle
vessel, reviewing the Fleet at
Spithead on the occasion of her
Diamond Jubilee in 1897.

98.   A later royal yacht, also
*Victoria and Albert*, in Grand
Harbour, Malta, during a visit
paid by King Edward VII and
Queen Alexandra to the Mediter-
ranean Fleet in 1904.

99.  Preparing light-cables aboard
HMS *Edinburgh*.

100.  Looking forward along the boat deck
of the battleship *Renown* where the ship's
boats were stowed in crutches abaft the two
large twin funnels; *c*. 1900.

101.   Divers preparing to descend.

102.   The first British submarine, launched at Barrow on 2nd October 1901, built to the design of the American inventor John Holland.

103.   Three of the earliest submarines in the Royal Navy lying alongside HMS *Hazard*, a torpedo gunboat acting as depot ship.

104.   Submarine No. 3 passes HMS *Victory* in Portsmouth Harbour with five of her crew of seven outside the hull.

105. The five Holland-type submarines were shortly followed by thirteen of the larger 'A' class, one of which is seen here in company with two cruisers.

106.   Submarine B8, one of a class of eleven
vessels, fitting out at Barrow in 1906.

107.   HM Submarine C11 ('C' class) with her
crew on deck, about 1908.

108.   The cruiser *Bonaventure* fitted out as
depot ship for a submarine flotilla.

109. The boys of HMS *Fisgard*, a training establishment for engine room artificers at Portsmouth, marching past the Commander-in-Chief, Portsmouth. The figurehead came from the *Royal Frederick*.

110. Where the sailor slung his hammock was his own affair and once he had secured his place he guarded it for all time. A story common in the Navy was told of an inexperienced ordinary seaman who slung his hammock in the cable locker, and one night when the Captain decided to anchor, the unfortunate O.S. found himself, wrapped round in his hammock, being whirled up to the deck, round the cable holder, along the forecastle, down the hawse pipe and into the cold North Sea.

111. 'Watch below' in the battleship *Alexandra*. Waking a sailor in the morning was undertaken by petty officers with strident voices among whose cries were the well-known 'Wakey Wakey', 'Show a leg, rouse and shine, the sun is a-scorching your eyeballs'.

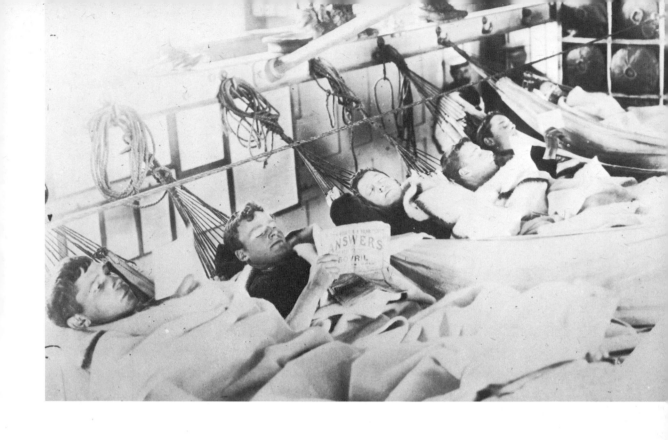

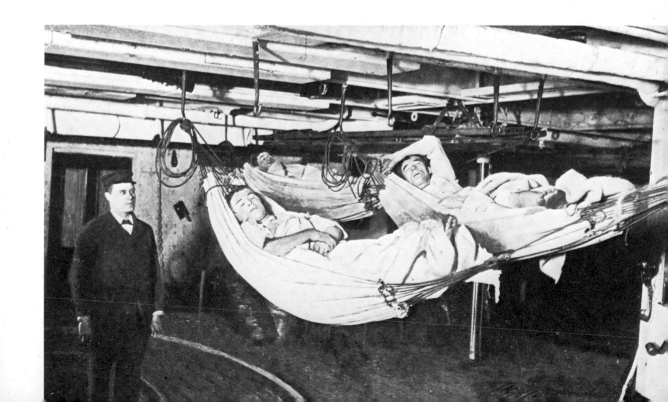

112. Serving out the day's fresh meat ration to the cooks of the various messes.

113. A yarn in the galley.

114. Dinner on the messdecks in the early days of this century. Each table constituted a separate mess. The table was suspended from the deckhead by steel bars, unshipped after each meal and scrubbed by two men from each mess who took it in turns for a duty of twenty-four hours. Although known as cooks of the mess these men merely collected the food from the galley and were responsible for the cleanliness of the mess and the washing of the plates.

115. The amount of room available for messing in warships has always been restricted. Here some ratings are messing in the lower battery.

116. Rum issue on board HMS *Edinburgh*. The daily issue of rum was made by petty officers responsible for seeing that only the right quantity was given to the representative of each of the many messes throughout the ship. Non-drinkers were given a small money allowance, which was recorded in a book. The rum was diluted, one part rum and three parts water, and this was known as 'grog' after Admiral Vernon, who introduced it into the Navy and was known as 'Old Grog' after his grogram boat cloak.

117. Soap and tobacco were issued regularly. They were in the charge of the ship's paymaster, in whose presence they were doled out.

118. The Navy has its own way with sailors who leave their possessions 'sculling about'. They are collected and stowed in a 'scranbag', the contents of which are sold by auction for the good of all.

119. For as long as there were rigged ships, laundry included sails as well as hammocks and individual clothing.

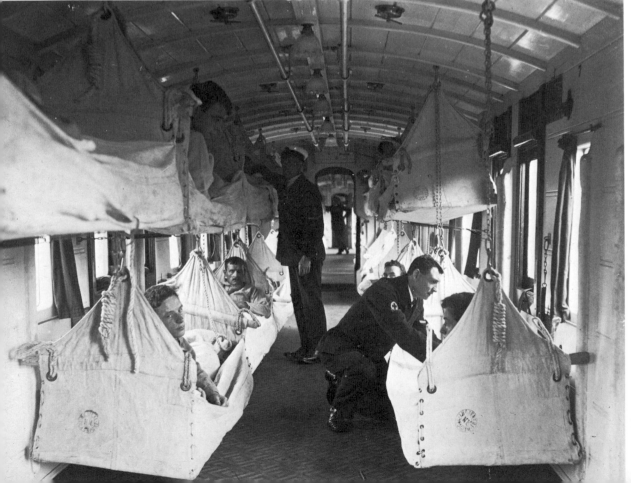

120.  Thursday Make and Mend on board. One afternoon a week was allotted to every sailor to make new articles of clothing and to keep his uniform in good repair.

121.  In the sick bay of a cruiser.

122.  A lieutenant (centre) with a cadet on his left and three midshipmen aboard a troop-ship en route to join their ship.

123.   The Captain comes aboard, greeted by the officer of the watch, a midshipman on duty and the bosun, who sounds his pipe, in his right hand, and salutes with his left.

124.   The Captain of a large warship had the option of feeding in the officers' mess (the ward room) or of dining alone or with his guests in his own quarters. The Captain of HMS *Sanspareil* entertaining the senior officers of his command, including the Commander and the captain of marines. In the ward room officers took turns to pay for the wine at dinner. In Nelson's flagship the two bottles used stood in a silver stand made in the form of a boat—hence the expression 'pushing out the boat' for standing drinks. The silver 'boat' may be seen today in the Nelson room at Lloyds in London.

125.   In the ward room of HMS *Magnificent*.

126.   Gun room of HMS *Temeraire*. The gun room of a warship is the home of the very junior officers.

127.   Cooks and stewards of a battleship in the Mediterranean.

128.   'Shooting the sun'. The officer of the watch checks the ship's position at midday with a sextant.

129.   The quarterdeck of an armoured cruiser with the officer of the watch at the accommodation ladder ready to receive visitors. With him are the duty midshipman, the bosun (with his pipe) on the extreme right, and side boys, one with a bugle and another with a telescope. The tampions in the muzzles of the 9·2-inch guns depict shamrock, as befits the ship's name, *Shannon*.

130.  The battleship *Royal Sovereign* about 1902, at anchor with her quarterdeck awning spread. The fighting tops on both masts contained 3-pounder quick-firing guns, and at the head of the mainmast may be seen the semaphore arms.

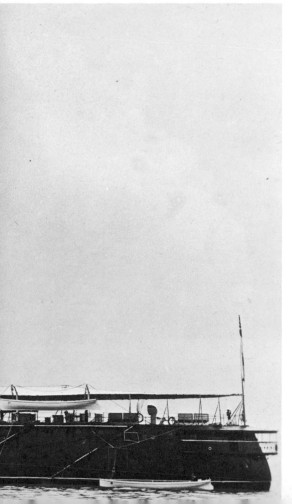

131.   In 1902 Russia sent the cruiser *Askold*, the only five-funnelled warship in the world, to the Persian Gulf; the Persians were considerably impressed. Britain ordered HMS *Amphitrite*, then on her way to the China Station, to proceed to Muscat. *Amphitrite*, an 11,000-ton first-class protected cruiser, was larger than *Askold* but had only four funnels, so the Captain rigged two extra funnels of wood and canvas and led smoke to them. Thus prestige was restored!

132.    Built at Greenock in 1878, the *Consuelo* was a handsome private steam yacht. In 1903 she was bought by the Admiralty and renamed *Skylark* for use as a surveying vessel.

133.  The steam sloop *Cadmus*, launched at Sheerness in 1903, was probably the last ship in the Navy to have a figurehead.

134–6. Naval brigades in training.
*Left above:* Disembarking a field gun. *Left below:* Storming the heights! *Below:* Holding a hastily contrived 'trench' with a Maxim gun and a light field gun.

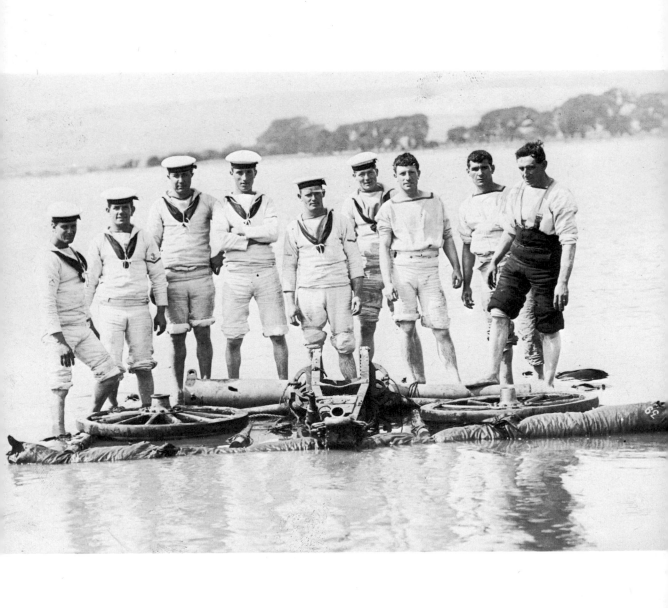

137–8.  Naval brigades in training.
Using an improvised raft to transport a gun
across a river. Cleaning the wheels of a gun
carriage after an operation ashore.

139.   In this re-enactment of the part played
by a Naval Brigade at the relief of Mafeking
may be recognized an early rehearsal of the
annual inter-team gun competition held at the
Royal Tournament of today.

140. At the end of 1903, just prior to the Russo-Japanese War, two battleships building in British yards for the Chilean Navy were purchased by the Admiralty to prevent their being acquired by Russia. They were renamed HMS *Swiftsure* and *Triumph*. Although successful ships, their foreign appearance made them unpopular. Each had two tall, widely spaced funnels and two goose-necked cranes, the latter visible in this photograph of the forecastle of *Triumph*, which also shows the shelters with machine gun on top at either end of the bridge; the *Swiftsure* had no such shelters.

141. The Admiralty started to experiment with oil fuel in 1900. Tests made with the destroyer *Surly* were so successful that it was decided to fit new vessels with a device to direct a spray of oil into the coal-burning furnaces when a burst of speed was called for.

142. HMS *Berwick*, a county class cruiser launched in 1902, here flying her church pendant, which dates back to the Anglo–Dutch wars of the seventeenth century.

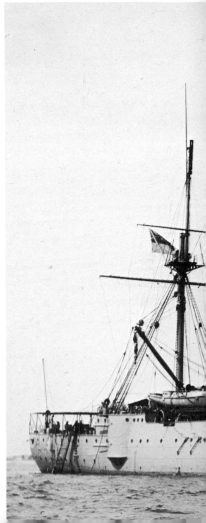

143, 144. As the anchor came up from the seabed the cable was often covered with mud and slime; before being stowed in the cable locker, the cable was hosed down and scrubbed by the anchor party as it was hauled along the forecastle and round the cable holder.

145. Changing a battleship's anchor cables: the old cable being laid into a dockyard barge. Studded cable—i.e. with bars or studs across the links—was used because it was stronger and did not kink.

146. HMS *Caesar*, one of the nine battleships of the Majestic class of the 1890s, shortly after she had hoisted the flag of the Rear Admiral, Second in Command of the Channel Fleet. At the head of the mainmast is the tall, thin gaff carrying the earliest wireless aerials.

147. HMS *Prince George* of the Majestic class, about 1904. This was the last class of battleship to have twin funnels side by side. Here members of her crew are using her starboard lower boom to come aboard from one of her boats.

148, 149.   In September 1904 one of the early torpedo-boat destroyers was lost as the result of an unusual accident. While HMS *Chamois* was proceeding at speed in a calm sea in the Gulf of Patras a propeller blade broke off and pierced the hull. Other destroyers of her flotilla came to her assistance and no lives were lost, although two stokers were severely scalded. She sank in thirty fathoms of water.

150.   Edward VII at Portsmouth selecting parts of the *Royal George*, including the figurehead, to be preserved and incorporated in future vessels. The *Royal George*, a former royal yacht, was broken up in 1905.

151. HMS *Commonwealth*, one of eight King Edward VII class battleships, each of which carried a main armament of four 12-inch, four 9·2-inch and ten 6-inch guns. They were satisfactory seaboats although very wet forward when steaming at moderate speed even in smooth water.

152. HMS *Dreadnought*, built in 1906. This historic battleship was the first capital ship to have a main armament of one calibre only, ten 12-inch guns mounted in five turrets. She was also the first battleship to be driven by turbines, which gave her a speed of 21 knots. Her heavy tripod foremast and small tripod mainmast gave her a distinctive appearance.

153. The torpedo gunboat *Speedwell* escorting torpedo-boat destroyers at Pembroke, 1906.

154. For fourteen years HMS *Iphigenia* served as a cruiser on various stations until 1906, when she and two or three of her sister ships were converted into the Royal Navy's first minelayers. The mines were discharged from her stern and may be seen stowed along her deck just abaft her second funnel.

155. The early torpedo boat was of necessity a flimsy craft. In June 1907 while Torpedo Boat No. 99 was carrying out steam trials her stern tube broke and she sank; no lives were lost. Two months later she was raised and beached near Brixham but broke in two. The forepart was towed to Devonport followed shortly by the salvaged afterpart. A partially rebuilt TB 99 was at sea again in February 1909.

156. On 25th April 1908 while the cruiser *Gladiator* was proceeding up the Solent she was struck amidships on the starboard side by the American liner *St Paul*; twenty-seven of her crew were killed. She was beached at Yarmouth, Isle of Wight, and after great efforts to salvage her she was refloated and towed to Portsmouth, but was considered too badly damaged to be repaired.

157. The funeral of the men killed in the *Gladiator* was attended by a naval landing party clad in gaiters, belts and sidearms, and wearing the popular straw hats worn in summer time up to the First World War.

158. Built at Dumbarton in 1900 as a commercial vessel and bought by the Navy, the paddle-wheel river gunboat *Kinsha* joined the force patrolling the Yangtse-Kiang, where this photograph was taken in 1909.

159. The destroyers of the River class, to which HMS *Boyne* belonged, were the first in the British Navy to have raised forecastles and no turtle decks.

160, 161. HMS *Good Hope* was one of four armoured cruisers of the Drake class. These ships were armed with sixteen 6-inch guns mounted in four double casemates sponsoned out on either side of the ship, and two 9·2-inch guns in single barbettes, one on the forecastle and the other on the quarterdeck. The stern-walk gave privacy to the commanding officer, since the walk was not visible from other parts of the ship.

162. In July 1909 the Fleet visited the Thames, the large ships lying off Southend. By Tower Bridge were the torpedo gunboat *Hazard* and the destroyer *Moy* with submarine C15 alongside. Londoners came out in small boats to view this unusual sight.

163. The new king of Portugal, Manoel, being saluted by a guard of honour on his arrival in the royal yacht *Victoria and Albert* for a few days' visit to England in 1909.

164–8. Coaling was at all times a hard and exceedingly grimy job. The 'super-Dreadnought' *Neptune*, launched in 1909, had a normal capacity of 900 tons and a total capacity of 2,710 tons, and the Herculean task of taking on a full load in small baskets carried by hand, as here at Gibraltar, occupied the full exertions of almost all the ship's crew and many of her officers from dawn to dusk and often for most of the night as well. Interest in the operation was kept up by communiques showing how many tons had already been stowed. Often the work was cheered along by a ship's amateur band.

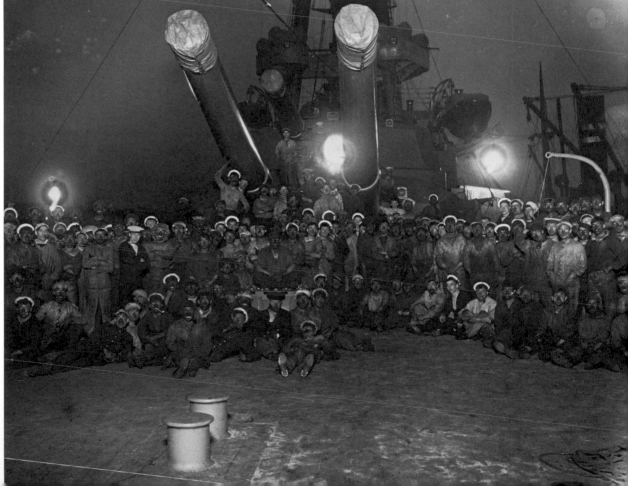

169. Going below to trim the bunker.

170. Early in 1910 the [de]stroyer *Eden* parted her m[oor]ings during a gale and [was] driven onto the sea wal[l at] Dover. At low tide she [was] high and dry and seen t[o be] badly damaged. She was [re]floated and is seen here be[ing] examined in dock at Dove[r.]

171. The cruiser *Melampus* was one of the ships built as a result of the Naval Defence Act of 1889. She spent most of her naval life around the shores of the United Kingdom and in her early days was commanded by the future King George V. She is here seen being towed to the breaker's yard in 1910.

172. HMS *Formidable*, one of the sturdy pre-*Dreadnought* battleships, photographed in 1912. The two men working on the lower yard of the foremast are supported by the foot rope fitted for this purpose. The ship's picquet boat, a steam vessel, lies tied to the lower boom.

173.  The first three battle cruisers of the
Royal Navy, the *Indomitable* (shown here),
*Inflexible* and *Invincible* (Pl. 186), all
launched in 1907, were cruiser editions of
HMS *Dreadnought*. They had one turret
less and were less heavily armoured but
were longer and had a speed advantage of
some four knots. They made all earlier
armoured cruisers obsolete.

174. HMS *Cyclops* was a repair ship built in 1905. She was fitted with foundries, machine tools, distilling apparatus and tanks for 800 tons of distilled water. Among the services she performed was towing targets, such as the one seen here lashed to her side, to sea for gunnery practice; about 1912.

175. Torpedo nets, fitted to all the Edwardian and early George V battleships, were suspended on booms (visible in several photographs) which were swung out at right angles to the hull. They cut down a ship's speed drastically and were of little service when she was under way; they were discontinued when war came in 1914 (see also Pl. 39).

176. The last warship to be built in London, HMS *Thunderer*, an Orion class super-Dreadnought, enters the water at Blackwall from the yard of the Thames Ironworks on 1st February 1911.

177. A complicated drill to raise or lower the seaboats is executed at the double. Here the crew of the battleship *Marlborough* are manning the long ropes by which each boat is hauled from sea level to the davits, the time beaten out for them by the Royal Marine band. The exercise is apparently being filmed.

178. During a visit by the King to the First and Second Fleets at Weymouth in May 1912 the battleship *Hibernia* made history by being the first British warship from which a seaplane had ever taken off while the ship was under way. A platform was erected over the forecastle from the bows to the forward superstructure, from which was flown a Short biplane, which circled the Fleet.

179. Later in the year HMS *London* took over the special equipment for launching seaplanes, which took off by means of small wheeled trolleys attached to the floats that fell away as the plane became airborne. The planes had to land on the sea, and were winched back on board.

180. Battleships of the Majestic class, a cruiser and several destroyers in the enclosed harbour at Dover, about 1912. The harbour had been opened in 1907.

181. The Orion class battleships, all completed in 1912, were armed with ten 13·5-inch guns mounted in five turrets on the centre line. On the side of HMS *Conqueror* can here be seen a Night Life Buoy, a contraption which floated and showed a self-ignited calcium flare; a spirit ration and a whistle were carried in one of the copper globes.

182. A Dreadnought dry-docked: HMS *Monarch* (Orion class) out of the water for a survey.

183. The Clyde-built battle cruiser *Australia* leaving Portsmouth on completion in July 1913 to become flagship of the recently established Royal Australian Navy.

184. On 21st December 1912 the destroyer *Beaver* stranded during a fog near Great Yarmouth. She was undamaged except for a slight dent in her bows and was refloated the same day.

185. On 28th July 1914 the L class destroyer *Laverock*, while completing her trials in the Clyde, made a turn at high speed and ran ashore, tearing a rent 45 feet long in her port side. She was refloated a month later and taken to Glasgow for repair.

186. An extra fifteen feet being fitted to the foremost funnel of HMS *Invincible* at Gibraltar early in 1915. Her sister ships *Indomitable* (Pl. 173) and *Inflexible* had been similarly treated in 1910 and 1911, for smoke and fumes from the funnel interfered considerably with men working on the bridge and upperworks.

187. The last peacetime social occasion attended by the Royal Navy before the outbreak of war was the ceremonial opening of the Kaiser Wilhelm Canal at Kiel in June 1914. The battleships *Audacious*, *Ajax*, *Centurion* and *King George V* (background) and the cruisers *Nottingham*, *Birmingham* and *Southampton* were visited by the Kaiser, who went on board the flagship, *King George V*.

188, 189.   The threat of war hung over the
Naval Review at Spithead in July 1914. These
small portions of the battle fleets shortly to
proceed to their wartime base at Scapa Flow
include (*above*) at left, battleships of the
Orion class, with *Orion* almost obscured by
the older *Collingwood* in line astern of her
Dreadnought-class sister ships with, beyond
them, vessels of the King George V class.
*Below*: HMS *Agamemnon*, *Bellerophon*, *Temeraire* and others.

190.  The strikingly graceful lines of the battle cruiser *Tiger*, launched in December 1913 and completed in October 1914.